beyond your number

an enneagram journal
to guide you forward
with greater wholeness

Type 3

Stephanie J Spencer

Certified Enneagram Coach
stephaniejspencer.com

with special thanks to

Ashley M Leusink
for graphic design and layout support
find out about her work as a spiritual director at
jesusandgin.com

Rachel McCauley
for copyediting support
find out about her work at
linkedin.com/in/rachel-d-mccauley

this journal is dedicated to

my family
who supports me, laughs with me, loves me,
and has been patient with me in the messy process
of finding my way as an enneagram coach.

my friends
who nerd out with me in enneagram conversations,
help me stay grounded and connected,
and remind me of the power of human belonging.

my clients
who teach me what it is to live as their enneagram types,
and give me wisdom to pass along
to others in my work.

Dear Reader,

Enneagram is not a personality test. It is a tool that gives insight into who we are and why we do what we do. These insights are intended to help us move forward in wholeness, freeing us from the passions and fixations of our types.

But knowing how to break out of these confines can prove difficult. We read books, listen to podcasts, follow Instagram accounts, and are left with the question, "Now what?"

The work can be daunting. This journal is meant to guide you through the forward movement of enneagram.

Its questions are designed to open space for you to see your behaviors, motivations, fears, and hopes with more clarity and compassion. The more honest we are with ourselves, the more insight we have into what practices might help us move forward in wholeness.

Growth is more like a wide and rocky river to navigate than a narrow set of steps to climb. Two people who are the same enneagram type may need to focus on vastly different areas of change. Our paths toward greater wholeness will be as diverse and unique as our backgrounds. Therefore, this journal is meant to be worked through as a winding path, taking you where you believe you need to go. It is not a fixed path from Point A to Point B.

The place where one person begins could be an ending place for another. The work you have already done might be the work someone else needs to begin.

I hope you will look through this journal, and allow questions to "rise from the page." The question that sticks out to you now is the one to sit with today. Answer it. Let a new question rise off the page when you are ready. Go at your own pace. Stay with a question as long as necessary: a day, a week, or a month. There isn't a right or a wrong pace.

However you engage with this journal, I hope it helps you on your journey of becoming the best version of you.

In hope,
Stephanie

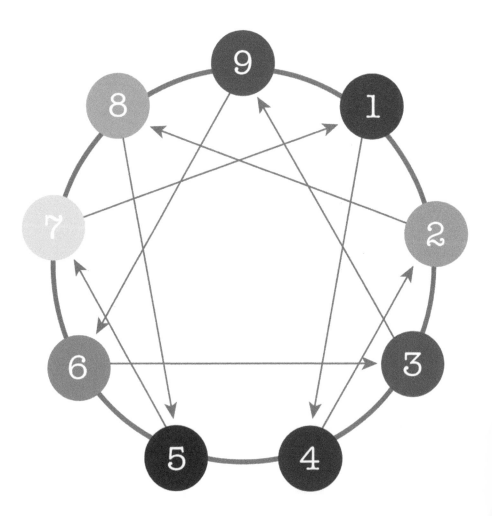

an enneagram overview

Enneagram is a framework that gives us insight into nine primary ways people engage in the human experience. These nine numbers are the enneagram types. The symbol that holds these numbers is a visual picture of the energy and interaction of the types. It is a framework that holds both complexity and unity, allowing us to be both a lot like other people and uniquely ourselves.

The circle reminds us we are all connected. We hold and display all numbers to some extent. However, we rest in one number as our home-base.

Our home-base enneagram type is the lens through which we see and experience the world.

When we know our type, we find language for the underlying factors that motivate us. We think about things like what we are afraid of, what we desire, and what makes us feel vulnerable. Knowing our enneagram number helps us name our shadows with compassion and take steps to live more deeply into our gifts.

No enneagram type is better or worse than another type. This is why numbers are more helpful than titles. As soon as we add words, there are things we do and don't want to be.

All nine enneagram types carry important facets of what it means to be human.

Each type is more of a spectrum than a point. We draw on the numbers next to our type as well, often drawing on one more strongly than the other. These adjacent numbers are called our wings.

Numbers connected to us by lines reflect our movement toward other types. In stressful states, we move with the arrow, compelled toward behaving like that type. In relaxed or secure states, we move against the arrow, opening to receiving the energy of the other type moving toward us.

Our enneagram number and its connected points are all important parts of who we are. We need to learn how to move in and receive the energies of each of them in order to move forward in wholeness.

recommended resources

This guided journal is meant to be a resource for those who already know their enneagram type and are familiar with the system. If enneagram is new to you, or you want to learn more, here are some places to explore.

websites

integrative9.com

enneagraminstitute.com

drdaviddaniels.com

podcasts

The 27 Subtypes of the Enneagram by The Liturgists

Typology with Ian Morgan Cron

The Enneagram Journey by Suzanne Stabile

music

Atlas: Enneagram by Sleeping at Last

primers

Enneagram Spectrum of Personality Styles by Jerome Wagner

The Road Back to You by Ian Morgan Cron and Suzanne Stabile

Enneagram Magazine Issue #1

deeper dives

The Complete Enneagram by Beatrice Chestnut

The Enneagram in Love and Work by Helen Palmer

The Sacred Enneagram by Chris Heuertz

The Wisdom of the Enneagram by Don Riso and Russ Hudson

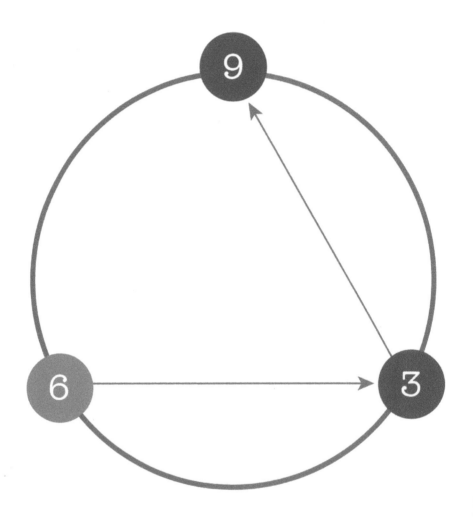

an overview of Type 3

Enneagram Type 3s have a natural ability to be successful. Their instincts guide them in how to have a positive image and achieve their goals in a variety of situations. Type 3s are energetic and motivated towards productivity. Their success can serve as a trap, however, as their self image becomes based on how they perform and produce. They sometimes deceive themselves and others as they show you not who they really are, but who they think you want to see.

As they connect into being instead of only doing, Type 3s display the virtue of authenticity. Their inner and outer image match, and they are honest about their strengths and weaknesses. They become loyal, trustworthy, and effective leaders.

When Type 3s feel stress, they connect with the energy of Type 9, which might look like being more stubborn, comfort-seeking, or mediating.

When Type 3s feel secure, they connect with the energy of Type 6, which might look like being more watchful, cooperative, or responsible.

why red?

Type 3s surveyed thought red was a good color to represent them, since it is a bold hue not afraid to be seen.

Red is an energetic color that also represents passion, a perfect combination for symbolizing the drive for achievement inside Type 3s.

Red can be a stressful color; an emotion Type 3s need to watch for in themselves as they try to do too much. Perhaps in those times, red can serve as reminder to cease and rest, just as a stop sign would call us to do.

Type 3s are part of the Assertive Triad, matched in brightness by the colors of Type 7 (yellow) and Type 8 (orange) on the enneagram symbol. These three types are the most independent and energetic. They want to take charge of their environments.

When Type 3s feel secure, they access the calm and loyal blue of the Type 6. This perhaps brings a bit of violet tone, still visible, but not overpowering.

To be nobody but
yourself in a world
which is doing its best day and night
to make you like everybody else
means to fight the hardest battle
which any human being can fight
and never stop fighting.

e.e. cummings

Enneagram is a map and a guide.
It does not describe the entire geography of the human landscape. It is meant to help us grow in awareness and move towards health and wholeness. It is not intended to hold every nuance and attribute of a human person.
I am an enneagram type.
I am ALSO a unique individual.

In what ways does enneagram Type 3 describe me?

In what ways does enneagram Type 3
not describe me?

How can I keep the tensions between my uniqueness
and enneagram Type 3 in mind as I do this work?

Are there any potential barriers keeping me from
doing the work of the enneagram?

Can I remove some of these barriers
before diving deeper?

What resources do I need in order to engage in the work of the enneagram? (i.e. intentional time)

Are there concrete supports that would help me move forward? (i.e. a friend with whom to process)

What is making me feel vulnerable, defensive, or afraid right now?

Do any of these things need to be resolved before moving forward with this journal?

Can I look at my habits with compassion
and choose to change them to reflect the values
true to my essence?

What might keep me from seeing myself with hope,
possessing the potential for change?

Can I use the enneagram as a tool to become more embodied and present to my life and relationships?

Can I keep this posture and goal in mind as I keep moving forward?

Are there ways I am trapped within
my enneagram type?

How do I need to recognize the transformation I have
already done before beginning the work of this
journal?

words that can be used to describe Type 3

productive   charming   role model

ambitious   image-conscious   performing

arrogant   appropriate   efficient

visionary   successful   competent

pragmatic   recognition-seeking   successful

workaholic   team player   enthusiastic

popular   goal-oriented   identifying

busy   impatient   dynamic

marketing   trendy   outgoing

scheming   motivated   strategic

What are three words I like?

What are three words I don't like?

What are three words that once
described me but no longer do?

What are three words that describe me now?

The life I am living
is not the same
as the life that wants
to live in me.

Parker Palmer

on image

What image do I show to others?

In what places is this image revealing my true self?

In what places is my image most distant from the truth?

What are the differences in the environments that make me feel more or less safe to be honest about my true self?

Can I tell the difference between what
I am successful at and what I want to do?

What would help me get more in touch with the
vulnerability of authentic desire?

What would it take for me to reveal more of my true self?

What do I fear? What holds me back?

Where am I seeking status?

How is this affecting my actions?

Why do I want it?

What would it take to feel like I am enough, regardless of what I achieve?

How do I set my feelings aside in order to get work done?

Would my actions change if I let my feelings have a place at the table?

How can I get more in touch with my heart?

What is holding me back from this work?

How does failure (or risk of failure)
make me feel vulnerable?

How has this affected my choices?

How does my leadership and drive
make the world better?

Can I celebrate the positive contributions I have
already made before I move to the next task?

on leadership

How has my ability to multi-task, achieve, and
be efficient led to success?

How do I feel about these achievements?

How have I used my ability to make things happen
to serve the greater good?

Have I felt pressure to step in and lead when
I really needed to step back and follow?

Where am I offering a performance
and where I am offering presence?

Are there ways and places I could show up
with a more vulnerable and sacrificial spirit?

Am I treating others
like my competition?

Is there something that could help me
see them more fully?

Authenticity is a collection of choices that we have to make every day. It's about the choice to show up and be real. The choice to be honest. The choice to let our true selves be seen.

Brené Brown

on accolades

Are there things I am doing because I want
to impress others?

Do I think I am good enough without trying
hard to be seen in a good light?

Where and how am I setting myself up to be a winner?

Have I avoided situations or projects that held risk
I might not be recognized as successful?

When is the last time I did something good for someone else, and kept that act a secret?

Do I speak to myself with kindness and compassion? Why or why not?

What would make me to feel loved and valued today?

How is my worth tied to my achievement?

To what extent do I believe who I am is different from what I do?

Has my ability to focus on and plan toward
goals helped myself or others achieve
important things? How?

Am I willing to sacrifice my own goals for the needs
of others? Who? When? How?

Are there times I have run over others
in pursuit of my goals?

Have I gone back to make amends
for these choices?

What are some ways I see productivity valued and
reflected in my life?

How might it affect my life if I also valued and
carved out space for rest?

Has my focus on efficiency and task overshadowed my investment in relationships? How?

When have I adapted and achieved in a way
that has helped a community?

Listen to your life. See it for the fathomless mystery that it is. In the boredom and pain of it no less than in the excitement and gladness: touch, taste, smell your way to the holy and hidden heart of it because in the last analysis all moment are key moments, and life itself is grace.

Frederick Buechner

Our first response to stress tends to be
to "double down" in our primary type.

In higher levels of stress, Type 3 moves toward Type 9.
The movement can be unhealthy or healthy,
paralyzing or resourcing.

Words that might describe a Type 9 include
patient, easygoing, calm, reassuring, neglectful, mediating,
conflict-avoiding, tedious, stubborn, flexible, comfort-seeking,
permissive, settled, distractible, supportive, grounded, low-energy

When I feel stress, do I get more productive, sell my image, seek
recognition, or display other stereotypical traits of Type 3?

Are there times when stress has made me feel like
a "different person"?

In stress, am I slipping into the less healthy characteristics of Type 9 and

... avoiding a problem that needs to be faced?

... dropping to exhaustion after running myself into the ground?

...giving up on my natural problem efficacy and becoming resigned to the way things are?

... seeking to numb through alcohol, food, sex, work, entertainment, or sleep?

In stress, am I connecting with the healthier characteristics of a Type 9 and

... slowing down to become more receptive and calm?

... taking action not based on successful outcome but on the greater good?

... dropping my mask and operating with less pretense?

... seeing the needs and perspectives of those around me with greater clarity?

Integrating my inner Type 9 will help me move forward in wholeness.

Can I consciously open myself to the healthier characteristics of this type?

When I feel secure, I may feel or act differently than I do at other times, and even from the typical descriptions of my enneagram type.

In security, Type 3 moves toward Type 6.
The movement can be unhealthy or healthy, paralyzing or resourcing.

Words that might describe a Type 6 include
cooperative, rigid, tenacious, responsible, vigilant, skeptical, cautious, prepared, loyal, dogmatic, worried, insightful, respectful, defensive, practical, rule-challenger, rule-follower

Some people might feel secure on a day off, or on vacation, or at home, or with a trusted friend.

What helps me feel secure?

In security, am I slipping into the less healthy
characteristics of a Type 7 and

... becoming overly compliant to please a group?

... putting myself above the rules and justified actions others
would perceive as wrong?

... taking on too many responsibilities in order to
prove my worth?

In security, when am I connecting with the healthier characteristics of a Type 6 and

... becoming loyal to myself and gotten in touch with who I really am?

... doing what is worthwhile and good even if it will not be seen or recognized?

... moving toward others in service to them instead of in my own self interest?

... submitting myself to the objective laws of the universe?

Integrating my inner Type 6 will help me move forward with wholeness.

Can I consciously open myself to the healthier characteristics of this type?

This above all: to thine ownself be true.

And it must follow, as the night the day,

Thou canst not then be false to any man.

William Shakespeare, Polonius in Hamlet

How have I cultivated my presence to carry
congruence and truth between
what I experience and what I express?

forward with wholeness

Are others experiencing the virtue of
authenticity emanating from my heart?

How do I inspire others through the way I live?

How is my life reflecting the reality of
the human experience?

How is vulnerability connecting me to love and worth?

How am I offering the gifts of hope and integrity
to the world?

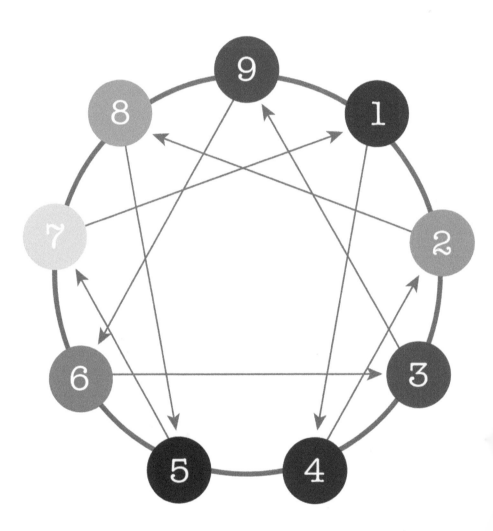

now what?

The question at the beginning of this journal re-surfaces. You have read books, listened to podcasts, perused websites, and followed Instagram accounts. Additionally, you have worked through this journal. I hope what you've written here will continue to be a reference that leads you to better, more complete versions of yourself.

But the question remains... now what?

Keep moving forward. It takes continual work to stay aware of ourselves. This world has a tendency to lull us to sleep.

Actively keep the characteristics, habits, and passions of your Type in your mind as you move through daily choices. Celebrate ways you have grown and notice where you still have room to move forward.

Take time to learn about numbers other than your own. Notice ways other Types exist in some way within you. If there is work to do there, open yourself up to it. (This may be especially useful with your stress response and security numbers.)

Ask the people in your life about their Types, and notice the similarities and differences in how you experience the world. Use enneagram as a tool to help you grow in compassion towards others.

Breathe. Be. Stay in touch with your body. Ground your questions with presence.

You may want to keep this journal to look at once or twice a year. Notice how your answers change. Celebrate the journey.

And if you get discouraged, maybe you can take with you one of my favorite quotes, from Parker Palmer,

"What a long time it can take to become the person you've always been."

From one becomer to another,
Stephanie

CPSIA information can be obtained
at www.ICGtesting.com
Printed in the USA
LVHW050905191020
669148LV00009B/316